Unafraid

Children's Leader Guide

Unafraid:
Living with Courage and Hope in Uncertain Times

Unafraid
978-1-5247-6033-5 *Hardcover*
978-1-5247-6034-2 *e-Book*

Unafraid: DVD
978-1-5018-5375-3

Unafraid: Leader Guide
978-1-5018-5373-9
978-1-5018-5374-6 *e-Book*

Unafraid: Youth Leader Guide
978-1-5018-5382-1
978-1-5018-5383-8 *e-Book*

Unafraid: Children's Leader Guide
978-1-5018-5384-5

Also from Adam Hamilton

24 Hours That Changed the World
Christianity and World Religions
Christianity's Family Tree
Confronting the Controversies
Creed
Enough
Faithful
Final Words from the Cross
Forgiveness
Half Truths
John
Leading Beyond the Walls
Love to Stay
Making Sense of the Bible
Moses
Not a Silent Night
Revival
Seeing Gray in a World of Black and White
Selling Swimsuits in the Arctic
Speaking Well
The Call
The Journey
The Way
Unleashing the Word
When Christians Get It Wrong
Why?

For more information, visit www.AdamHamilton.org

UNAFRAID

LIVING WITH COURAGE AND HOPE IN UNCERTAIN TIMES

ADAM HAMILTON

Children's Leader Guide
by Susan Groseclose

Abingdon Press / Nashville

Unafraid:
Living with Courage and Hope in Uncertain Times
Children's Leader Guide

This book is printed on elemental chlorine-free paper.
ISBN 978-1-5018-5384-5

18 19 20 21 22 23 24 25 26 27 — 10 9 8 7 6 5 4 3 2 1
MANUFACTURED IN THE UNITED STATES OF AMERICA

Contents

To the Leader

This children's leader guide is designed for use with Adam Hamilton's book and program, *Unafraid: Living with Courage and Hope in Uncertain Times*. This guide includes five lessons that will help children face their fears and live unafraid. God gives us the gifts of courage, love, grace, hope, and peace to overcome our fears. Each week, the biblically based activities help children explore one of God's gifts and practice ways to live unafraid.

The lessons in this guide, designed for children in kindergarten through sixth grade, are presented in a large group / small group format. Children begin with time spent at activity centers, followed by time together as a large group. Children end the lesson in small groups determined by grade level. Each lesson plan contains the following sections:

Focus for the Teacher

The information in this section will provide you with background information about the week's lesson. Use this section for your own study as you prepare.

Explore Interest Groups

You'll find in this section ideas for a variety of activity centers. The activities will prepare the children to hear the day's Scripture. Allow the children to choose one or more of the activities that interest them.

Large Group

The children will come together as a large group to hear the Bible verses or story for the week. This section begins with a transition activity followed by the story, a Bible verse memory activity, and worship to conclude the large group time.

Small Groups

Children are divided into age-level groups for small group time. Depending on the size of your class, you may need to have more than one group for each age level. It is recommended that each small group contain no more than ten children.

Younger Children

The activities in this section are designed for children in grades K-2.

Older Children

The activities in this section are designed for children in grades 3-6.

Reproducible Pages

At the end of each lesson are reproducible pages, to be photocopied and used during the lesson.

Schedule

Many churches have weeknight programs that include an evening meal, an intergenerational gathering time, and classes for children, youth, and adults. The following schedule illustrates one way to organize a weeknight program.

5:30	Meal
6:00	Intergenerational gathering introducing weekly themes and places for the lesson. This time may include presentations, skits, music, and opening or closing prayers.
6:15–7:30	Classes for children, youth, and adults.

Churches may want to do this study as a Sunday school program. The following schedule takes into account a shorter class time, which is the norm for Sunday-morning programs.

10 minutes	Intergenerational gathering
45 minutes	Classes for children, youth, and adults

Choose a schedule that works best for your congregation and its Christian education programs.

Blessings to you and the children as you learn and practice how to be unafraid!

1 God Is the Giver of Courage

Objectives

The children will:

- name some of their fears.
- explore ways that God gave courage to the Israelites to enter into the Promised Land.
- practice facing their fears with courage.

Theme

We become unafraid when we receive God's gift of courage to face our fears with faith.

Bible Verse

Don't fear, because I am with you. (Isaiah 41:10)

Focus for the Teacher

Welcome to *Unafraid.* Young children commonly fear the dark, monsters, and animals, especially dogs. Older children often fear storms, being home alone, failure or rejection, illness (particularly doctor visits and shots), tragic news, and death. However, God gives us the gifts of courage, love, grace, hope, and peace to overcome our fears. At the beginning of each session, we will explore one of these gifts with a variety of games, crafts, and activities. During the large group time, the children will experience the day's Bible story and learn a memory verse. These memory verses will help children remember ways to not be afraid. Each session ends in age-level groups to practice ways of living unafraid.

Fear is a real, biologically based phenomenon. The amygdala is one of two almond-shaped structures nestled deep on each side of the brain. These structures, processing threats even before danger registers in our conscious mind, release hormones that signal the perceived threat. Biologically our impulse is to either fight or flee.

At times, fear can be a gift that motivates us to action, such as jumping out of the way of a moving object. However, these biological responses can also paralyze us to inaction, and sometimes the responses can be triggered by things that in fact are not threats, making us fearful for little or no reason.

The phrase *Do not be afraid* appears over a hundred times in the Bible, when God's people experience the type of fear that is not helpful.

Face our fears with faith.

The Israelites, after escaping Egypt, traveled in the desert for two years, finally arriving a mile from the Promised Land. They sent out twelve spies to determine whether to move forward. Two spies came back encouraging the Israelites onward, but the other ten spies told the Israelites they were too small to fight the people who looked like giants. The Israelites became afraid and remained in the desert. Thirty-eight years later, they received God's gift of courage and moved into the Promised Land.

We, too, are a fearful people. As you help children understand what it means to be unafraid, list some of the fears that children in your church have experienced. List some of your own fears. How have you and others in your church moved beyond fear and found courage? What Bible verses or hymns help when you are afraid?

Explore Interest Groups

Be sure that adult leaders are waiting when the first child arrives. Greet and welcome the children. Get the children involved in an activity that interests them and introduces the theme for the day's activities.

Do Not Be Afraid

- Pair the children. It will be helpful to pair an older child with a younger child.
- Give each child a copy of **Reproducible 1a: Do Not Be Afraid**.
- **Say:** The phrase *Do not be afraid* appears over one hundred times in the Bible. Look up each Bible verse listed in the left-hand column, and match that verse with the name of the person in the right-hand column who is told in the verse not to be afraid.
- After the pairs have finished their work, **ask:** Why were some of the people in the Bible afraid? What makes you afraid?
- **Say:** These next few weeks, we are going to be learning ways to not be afraid.

Prepare

✓ Photocopy for each child **Reproducible 1a: Do Not Be Afraid**, found at the end of the lesson.

✓ Provide pencils.

Giants and Grasshoppers

- **Say:** Today's Bible story tells us that some people seemed as big as giants and other people seemed small like grasshoppers.
- **Ask:** If you were a giant, would you be afraid of a grasshopper? If you were a grasshopper, would you be afraid of a giant? Why or why not?
- **Say:** There are cards in this basket. On some of the cards is the word giant, and on other cards is the word grasshopper. Each of you will come forward, pick a card, and then put it back into the basket face-down. If you pick a card with the word giant, tell us something that can be big and scary. If you pick a card with the word grasshopper, tell us something that might be small but scary.
- If needed, help the children come up with ideas.
- **Say:** These next several weeks, we are going to learn how to be unafraid. We are going to learn what to do when we have big fears and when we have small fears.

Prepare

✓ Before class, write on four index cards the word *giant*, and on four index cards the word *grasshopper*. Place the cards face down in a basket and mix them up.

Prepare

- ✓ Provide smooth stones, acrylic paint in a variety of colors, and clear gloss.
- ✓ Use newspapers or drop cloths to cover tables or the floor where children will be painting.
- ✓ You may want to get aprons or some old extra-large T-shirts for the children to wear over their clothes while painting.

Courage Stones

- **Say:** Today we are going to make a courage stone. You'll paint a rock your favorite color, or you can use different colors to paint a design on your rock.
- Let each child choose a rock.
- Show the children the paint colors and paint area, and tell them they can begin painting their courage stones.
- After children are finished, spray the rocks with clear gloss to protect their designs, and set the stones aside.
- **Say:** Over the next several weeks, we will be talking about our fears.
- **Ask:** When have you been afraid?
- **Say:** Today, we are going to hear how God gave the Israelites courage when they were afraid. We will leave the stones here to dry. At the end of class, you can take your courage stone home. Whenever, you are afraid, hold the courage stone in your hand. Remember that God gives us courage to be unafraid.

Large Group

Bring all the children together to experience the Bible story. Use a bell to alert the children to the large group time.

What Am I?

- Have the children sit in a circle.
- Put the map on the floor or table in the middle of the circle.
- **Ask:** What do you remember about Moses?
- **Say:** This map shows the Exodus journey of Moses and the Israelites.
- Divide the children into six groups, with older and younger children in each group.
- Give each group one of the cards containing a riddle.
- **Say:** Work with your group to read the Bible verse on the card, answer the riddle, and write the answer on the card.
- After the groups have found their answers, have each group share their riddle and answer.
- Help the children locate their answers on the map and tape their cards to it.
- **Say:** Our Bible story today is about Moses and the Israelites' journey through the Sinai Desert.

Prepare

✓ Copy or print out a map of the Exodus journey from a children's Bible or the Internet.

✓ Copy **Reproducible 1b: What Am I?** on a piece of card stock and cut out the six cards, each of which contains a riddle.

✓ Provide Bibles and tape.

God Gives Us Courage

- **Ask:** When have you been afraid?
- **Say:** God gives us gifts to help us when we are afraid. Today, we are going to talk about God's gift of courage.
- **Ask:** What does *courage* mean? What are some ways you can show courage?
- Encourage the children's ideas.
- **Say:** Today I'm going to read you a story about when Moses and the Israelites were afraid. Listen for what happened when they had courage. Whenever I say, "God gives us courage," I'd like you to repeat it.
- Read the story on **Reproducible 1c: God Gives Us Courage**, pausing after "God gives us courage" so children can repeat it.
- **Ask:** Why were the Israelites afraid? When were they courageous? What do you think they should have done when they heard the spies' reports?

Prepare

✓ The leader will need a copy of **Reproducible 1c: God Gives Us Courage**, found at the end of the lesson.

Prepare

✓ Provide a markerboard, marker, and eraser.

✓ Write at the top of the board the day's Bible verse: "Don't fear, because I am with you" (Isaiah 41:10).

God Is with Us

- **Say:** Each week, we are going to learn a Bible verse that helps us be unafraid. You can memorize these verses and remember them whenever you are afraid.
- Together with the class, read this week's Bible verse from the board.
- Below the Bible verse, draw a vertical line down the board.
- Title one side "Israelites" and the other side "Us."
- **Ask:** What are some ways that God was with the Israelites when they were afraid?
- List the children's answers under "Israelites."
- **Ask:** How is God with us when we are afraid?
- List the children's answers under "Us."
- **Ask:** How are these two lists the same? How are they different?
- **Say:** God was with the Israelites, and God is always with us. God is with us when we are afraid. God gives us courage and shows us how to be unafraid.
- Read this week's Bible verse together again.
- **Say:** To help us memorize the verse, I'll erase one word at a time and see if you can still remember the verse.
- Erase one word at a time, and each time recite the entire verse with the class, including the missing word. Continue doing this until all the words are erased and the children can recite the verse from memory.

Prepare

✓ Print out copies of the words for the hymn "Guide My Feet" from a hymnal or the Internet, so there is one copy per child.

Courage, Not Fear

- **Say:** Whenever we pray, we can ask God to guide us. We can ask God to give us courage so that we will not be afraid. Sometimes, we may even sing our prayer.
- Hand out the words to "Guide My Feet" and either sing or recite the first verse together.
- **Say:** We can change the words to talk about being unafraid: "Guide my feet when I am afraid . . . for I don't want to be afraid today!"
- Sing or recite the hymn again using the new words. You may repeat the first verse several times or go on to the additional verses: "Hold my hand when I am afraid," "Stand by me when I am afraid," and so forth.
- Dismiss children to their small groups.

Small Groups

Divide the children into small groups. You may organize the groups around age levels or around readers and nonreaders. Keep the groups small, with a maximum of ten children in each group. You may need to have more than one group at each age level.

Young Children

- Have the children sit at tables.
- **Say:** Today we are going to make a cross. We remember that God is always with us, particularly when we are afraid.
- Give each child two craft sticks.
- Glue the sticks in the shape of a cross.
- Use the buttons to decorate the front of the cross.
- Cut the yarn for a hanger.
- Loop the yarn into a hanger and glue on the back of the cross.
- **Say:** Take your cross home and hang it in your room. Remember that God is always with you even when you are afraid.
- Have the children stand in a circle.
- **Say:** God gives us courage when we are afraid.
- **Ask:** What can you do when you are afraid?
- Encourage and guide the children's answers: pray, talk to someone, remember our Bible verse, use a night-light in my room, and so forth.
- **Say:** We are going to pray with our bodies. Show me with your body how you have courage.
- Encourage the children to show different poses.
- **Say:** I am going to pray a sentence. Then you will show your courage and say, "I have courage."
- Practice one or two times in preparation for the prayer.
- **Pray:**

Thank you, God, for giving us courage when we are afraid.

I have courage.

Remind us to pray when we are afraid.

I have courage.

Remind us to talk with someone when we are afraid.

I have courage.

[Add sentences using the children's ideas. Then finish the prayer:]

Help us remember not to be afraid and that you are always with us.

I have courage.

Amen.

Prepare

✓ Provide craft sticks, glue, a variety of sizes and colors of buttons, and yarn.

Prepare

✓ Provide paper and pencils or pens.

Older Children

- Have the children sit in a circle.
- **Say:** It takes courage to face our fears and work to overcome them.
- Give each child a piece of paper and ask them to fold it in half.
- **Say:** On one half of the paper write something that you're afraid of or that you were afraid of, that you don't mind sharing with the group.
- Encourage children to write a fear. If needed, help them identify a fear.
- Have each child pass their paper to the person next to them on the right.
- **Say:** On the other half of the paper write something the person can do to overcome this fear.
- Pass the paper to the next person in the circle.
- **Say:** Write something else you can do to overcome this fear.
- Continue passing the paper around the circle until everyone has written on all the papers.
- Have the children return the papers to their original authors.
- **Say:** Sometimes we don't know what to do when we are afraid. Read the suggestions and pick one thing you can do to overcome your fear.
- Invite the children, if they are willing, to share their fear and the suggestion they will use to overcome their fear.
- **Say:** Thank you for sharing your fear. Remember that if one idea doesn't work, you can try another idea. We are going to close our session by learning a simple breath prayer that we can use when we are afraid.
- **Say:** The first line is a name for God. The second line is what we need from God. Let's pray, saying, "Powerful God, give me courage."
- Have the children repeat the phrase.
- **Say:** This is a silent prayer between you and God. When you breathe in, say "Powerful God," and when you breathe out, say "Give me courage."
- Let the children practice breathing in "Powerful God" and breathing out "Give me courage."
- Repeat this several times.
- **Say:** You can pray this way to God anytime, but especially when you are afraid. Go, remembering that God is always with us. Go, remembering that God wants us to be unafraid.

Do Not Be Afraid

Work with another person. Look up and read each Bible verse. Draw a line to match the person's name who is told "do not be afraid."

a. Genesis 15:1

b. Numbers 21:34

c. Joshua 10:8

d. Ruth 3:9–11

e. 2 Kings 1:15

f. Matthew 1:20

g. Matthew 28:1–5 [the women]

h. Luke 1:30

i. Acts 27:24

Ruth

Mary

Abraham/Abram [Abram is in the verse]

Joseph

Paul

Elijah

Joshua

Mary Magdalene and the other Mary (28:1)

Moses

Answers:
a. Abraham/Abram; b. Moses; c. Joshua; d. Ruth; e. Elijah; f. Joseph; g. Mary Magdalene and the other Mary; h. Mary; i. Paul

What Am I?

1.
I am the country where Pharaoh was king. What country am I? (Exodus 6:11)

2.
I am the land where Joseph allowed his family to live in Egypt. What land am I? (Genesis 45:9-10)

3.
I am the sea that Moses led the Israelites through to save them from Pharaoh's armies. What sea am I? (Hebrews 11:29)

4.
I am the desert that Moses and the Israelites wandered through for forty years. What desert am I? (Exodus 19:1)

5.
I am the river that Joshua led the Israelites through into the Promised Land. What river am I? (Deuteronomy 11:31)

6.
I am the land that God promised to the Israelites. What land am I? (Leviticus 25:38)

Answers: 1. Egypt; 2. Goshen; 3. Red Sea; 4. Sinai Desert; 5. Jordan River 6. Canaan

God Gives Us Courage

(Based on Numbers 13)

Moses courageously led the Israelites out of Egypt. Moses and the Israelites did not let their fear of King Pharaoh's armies stop them at the Red Sea.

God gives us courage!

The Israelites journeyed through the Sinai Desert for two years. When they were one mile from the land of Canaan, God said to Moses, "Send out twelve spies. Tell them not be afraid and to explore the land that I have promised."

God gives us courage!

The spies went to see whether the people there were strong or weak. They went to see if the land was rich or poor. Moses told them to be courageous.

God gives us courage!

After forty days, the spies returned. They told Moses, "It is rich, fertile land. However, the people are very powerful."

God gives us courage!

Two of the spies said, "We must not be afraid. We can enter the land, and God will be with us." The other ten spies said, "No! The people look like giants. We look like grasshoppers. We are afraid. We cannot fight these giants."

God gives us courage!

The Israelites heard the ten spies and were afraid. They did not enter into the new land, and so they lived in the Sinai Desert for thirty-eight more years. Joshua became their new leader. He was courageous. He led them across the Jordan River and into the new land of Canaan.

God gives us courage!

2 God Is the Giver of Love

Objectives

The children will:

- explore ways to love others, particularly those who are different from them.
- experience the story of the good Samaritan.
- practice loving others with acts of kindness.

Theme

We become unafraid of those who are not like us when we receive and use God's gift of love.

Bible Verse

Love your neighbor as yourself. (Luke 10:27)

Focus for the Teacher

Generally, children are not afraid of another person unless they have been bullied or threatened or abused. Fear of loving others can also occur if your community is experiencing violence or racial tensions. In these cases, allow the children's questions and comments to guide your discussions.

This session will focus on ways to love others, including those who are different from us. Children are familiar with the story of the good Samaritan. This story is about loving others even when we are busy or have other things to do. The Samaritan stopped, saw the man's need, and befriended him. Jesus loves us and told this story to teach us how to love and care for others.

This story is also about loving the "other"—the one who is not like us. Children know that some children are left out or bullied. They know that others are treated differently because of the color of their skin, their background, or their inabilities. Jesus teaches that the Samaritan is the example we should follow. Fear should not keep us from loving others. Rather, we are to love all of God's people.

Do not be afraid to love others.

As a teacher, you can affirm the different ways children befriend others and practice love of others. You can help children discover ways to love others through their acts of kindness.

What relationships do you have in your own life with people who are different from you? How do these relationships enrich your life? Find stories of people in your congregation or community who love others with compassion and justice. List different ways that you and the children in your group can share God's love by loving others.

Explore Interest Groups

Be sure that adult leaders are waiting when the first child arrives. Greet and welcome the children. Get the children involved in an activity that interests them and introduces the theme for the day's activities.

Beads of Love

- **Say:** God created us to be unique and different. Jesus teaches us that we are to love each person no matter how we are alike or how we are different.
- **Ask:** How are your family or friends like you? How are they different?
- **Say:** Today, we are going to create our own unique bracelet to remind us to love each other.
- Give each child a chenille stem.
- **Say:** String whatever color, shape, or design of beads that you would like onto your chenille stem. You might want to choose a bead that reminds you of each member in your family or each of your friends. You might want to add a bead to remind you to love others who are not friends yet. You might want to add a bead to remind you to love a person who is hard to love.
- When you complete your string of beads, twist the ends of the chenille stem together to create a bracelet.
- **Say:** No two bracelets are alike, just as no two people are alike. Remember that we are to love each other no matter what.

Prepare

✓ Provide chenille stems and beads of different colors, sizes, and designs.

Emoji Charades

- **Ask:** When have you been happy? When have you been sad? When have you been scared? What are you feeling today?
- Divide the children into two teams.
- **Say:** I have a basket of different emojis. One person from your team will pick out an emoji and act out the emotion to the team. The team will try to guess what emotion is being acted out. If the team guesses correctly, the team gets one point.
- Continue playing until the first team reaches five points.
- **Say:** Jesus teaches us how to love one another.
- **Ask:** How do you love another person when they are sad? How do you love another person when they are scared? How do you love another person when they are cranky?

Prepare

✓ Using an Internet search, find free printables of emojis. Print them on card stock and cut them out into cards. Put the cards face-down in a basket.

Loving Words

Prepare

✓ Provide a shoebox, sandpaper, cotton balls, index cards, and pencils or pens.

- **Ask:** What words or actions might show that you love another person? What words or actions might hurt another person?
- **Say:** Today we are going to learn how Jesus teaches us to love one another.
- Pass the sandpaper around the group.
- **Ask:** How do you describe the sandpaper?
- **Say:** Sometimes our words, like sandpaper, can be rough and can hurt. (*Hint*: Use words that the children used to describe the sandpaper.) These words can make us feel bad.
- Put the sandpaper away/on a table/out of the way.
- Pass the cotton balls around the group.
- **Ask:** How do you describe the cotton?
- **Say:** Sometimes our words can be soft, warm, and fuzzy. (*Hint*: Use words that the children used to describe the cotton.) These words can make us feel good.
- Place the cotton balls in a box.
- Divide the group into pairs, with each pair having one older child and one younger child.
- Make available to the children a stack of index cards and pencils or pens.
- **Say:** Think about words that we say that are loving. Write each word on an index card and put it in the box with the cotton balls.
- Assist children as needed.
- **Say:** Jesus teaches us to love others. When you talk to others this week, think about whether your words are hurtful or loving.

Acts of Kindness

Prepare

✓ Before class, cut apart the cards on **Reproducible 2a: Acts of Kindness,** found at the end of the lesson.

✓ Place the cards in a basket, face-down.

- **Say:** Today's Bible verse tells us to think about others rather than ourselves. When we are kind, we think about the other person. Acts of kindness are small acts that are done for no reason and usually without recognition.
- **Ask:** What are some ways you can be kind to another person?
- **Say:** I have a basket of cards that give different ways to show kindness to someone. Let's each draw a card and do the act of kindness sometime during this coming week.

Large Group

Bring all the children together to experience the Bible study. Use a bell to alert the children to the large group time.

Common or Different?

- Have the children stand in a circle.
- **Say:** I am going to make a statement. If the statement is true for you, go to the center of the circle and "high-five" others who are like you.
- Name things that several children in your group have in common: have a brother, have a sister, blue eyes, brown eyes, wearing something blue, pizza is your favorite food, play on a sport team, came to church today, and so forth. Be sure that everyone is able to go to the center at least once.
- Have the children sit in a circle.
- **Say:** There are many things we have in common with others. Not everyone went to the center of the circle each time, and so we are also different from others. In fact, the only thing we all have in common is that we came to church today.
- **Ask:** What other things do you have in common with children at school or in your neighborhood?
- Write the children's answers on the markerboard under "Common."
- **Say:** It is sometimes easy to love people who are like us—people we know, people we go to school or church with, people in our families.
- **Ask:** What are some ways you are different from others in your school or neighborhood?
- Write the children's answers on the markerboard under "Different."
- **Say:** We have different abilities. We look different. We act different. (Name other differences the children have identified.) Sometimes it's a little harder to love people who are different from us.
- **Ask:** Why are some children left out at school? Why are some people treated differently? Encourage and guide the children's answers.

Prepare

✓ Provide a markerboard and markers.

✓ Draw a line down the middle of the board. Label one side "Common" and the other side "Different."

Prepare

✓ The leader will need a copy of **Reproducible 2b: The Good Samaritan,** found at the end of the lesson.

Gift of Love

- **Say:** Jesus told a story about a Samaritan. He knew those who heard the story had a hard time loving Samaritans because of differences between the two groups.
- Assign children to act out the different characters in the story: Jesus, the legal expert, the robbers, the man who was hurt, the priest, the Levite, the Samaritan, and the innkeeper.
- Read the story from **Reproducible 2b: The Good Samaritan** while the children pantomime the story.
- **Ask:** When have you been hurt by another person's actions or words? When have you been too busy to help someone, like the priest or the Levite who didn't show love? When is it easy to show love? When is it hard to show love? Why was the Samaritan, who was different from Jesus' listeners, the hero in this story?
- **Say:** Jesus teaches us to love everyone, including those who are different from us.

Prepare

✓ Provide a markerboard and markers.

✓ Write on the markerboard the day's Bible verse, "Love your neighbor as yourself" (Luke 10:27), along with the incomplete sentence, "We love others when we . . ."

Love One Another

- **Say:** Each week, we are memorizing a Bible verse.
- **Ask:** Does anyone remember last week's memory verse?
- Help the children remember the verse: "Don't fear, because I am with you" (Isaiah 41:10).
- **Say:** Today's memory verse is easy to remember.
- Read together, "Love your neighbor as yourself."
- Have the children complete the sentence, "We love others when we..."
- **Ask:** How can you love others? **Ask further**: How can you love those who are different?
- List the children's ideas on the markerboard.
- Read together again: "Love your neighbor as yourself."
- Have the children stand in a circle.
- **Say:** I am going to say the first word of our memory verse. The person next to me will say the next word. We will continue repeating the verse until everyone has learned it.

Litany of Love

- **Say:** Jesus loves us and all the children of the world, no matter what we look like, no matter our age, no matter our abilities or inabilities, no matter what we say or how we act. Jesus loves us. Jesus also teaches us to love everyone in the same way. Before we move into our small groups, we're going to pray together.
- Review the children's ideas on the markerboard. Add any new ideas.
- **Say:** I am going to read a sentence, "We love others when we . . ." Then the group will respond, "Let us love one another." We call this a litany.
- **Pray** the litany together. (*Hint*: If the group has generated many ideas, group their ideas together.)
- Dismiss children to their small groups.

Prepare

✓ Provide the markerboard of ideas that the children listed in the previous activity.

Small Groups

Divide the children into small groups. You may organize the groups around age levels or around readers and nonreaders. Keep the groups small, with a maximum of ten children in each group. You may need to have more than one group at each age level.

Prepare

✓ Provide long strips of paper, pencils, baby food jars with lids, and bags of marbles.

✓ Write on a markerboard or a large piece of paper: "Love Others."

Young Children

- **Say:** Last week, we talked about how to be unafraid.
- **Ask:** Who remembers God's gift that we learned about last week? When have you had courage this week?
- Encourage the children's answers.
- **Say:** Today's gift is love. Jesus loves us and shows us how to love others.
- **Ask:** What chores do you have at home? What chores do you not like to do? Have you ever not done a chore because you were too busy doing something else?
- Have the children share their stories.
- **Say:** Sometimes we need to show God's love even when we would rather do something else.
- **Ask:** What are some ways that you can show love to your parents? What are some ways that you can show love to other members of your family? How can you show love to others this week?
- Brainstorm a list of ideas.
- Give each child a strip of paper, a pencil, and a small jar.
- Tell the children to write "Love Others" on their strip of paper, then curl the strip of paper and place it in the jar so they can see the message.
- Give each child a bag of marbles.
- **Say:** Take your jar home. When you do something to love another person, add a marble to your jar.
- Stand in a circle.
- Encourage each child to complete this sentence prayer: "Thank you, God, for . . ."
- Remind the children to add marbles to their jar this week for showing their love for God!

Older Children

- **Say:** Last week we talked about how to be unafraid.
- **Ask:** Who remembers God's gift that we learned about last week? When have you had courage this week?
- Encourage the children's answers
- **Say:** Today's gift is love. We should not be afraid to love others. God shows us how to love one another.
- **Ask:** When is it easy to show love to another person? When is it hard to show love to another person?
- **Say:** We are going to role-play some situations and think about how we can love and befriend others.
- Divide the group into pairs.
- Each pair draws a scenario from the basket.
- Encourage the pair to discuss how they can show a way to love or befriend another person in that situation.
- Have each pair act out their situation.
- **Say:** The decisions we make in our relationships show that we are not afraid to love others, particularly those who are not like us. Our parents, our teachers, and our friends also help us love others.
- **Ask:** What are some ways in which they can help us?
- Give each child an index card and pen. Have them write the names of three people they can count on to help them remember how to love others.
- **Say:** This week, do your best to love others, particularly those who are difficult to love. If you find yourself in a situation and don't know what to do, talk with your parents or a teacher or a friend, and together figure out how you can love that person.
- **Pray:**

  Loving Christ, you show us how to love and care for others. Show us how to love even when we don't like another person. Show us how to love even when we would rather do something else. God, thank you for adults and friends who encourage us. Help us show your love to others. Help us befriend those who are difficult to love. Amen.

Prepare

✓ Copy **Reproducible 2c: Role-Play Scenarios,** found at the end of this lesson. Cut out each scenario, fold it, and place it in a basket.

✓ Provide index cards and pens.

Reproducible 2a

Acts of Kindness

Write a compliment on a sticky note and leave it where the person will find it.	Give a high-five and talk to to someone who is new in class.	Help a teacher clean up after an activity.
Call an older person in the congregation.	Write a letter or draw a picture telling your parents how much you love them.	Tell someone you are sorry.
Smile at someone across the room.	Give a hug to a friend and tell them why you like them.	Say hello to someone you have never spoken to.
Design a coupon promising to take out the garbage.	Design a coupon promising to wash the dishes.	Hold the door open for someone.
Create a card. Mail it to someone in your congregation.	Find a staff person at church and thank them for their service.	Let someone go ahead of you in line.

The Good Samaritan
(Based on Luke 10:25-37)

A legal expert asked Jesus. "Teacher, what must I do to faithfully follow you?"

"You must love the Lord your God with all your heart, with all your being, with all your strength, and with all your mind, and love your neighbor as yourself."

But the legal expert asked Jesus, "And who is my neighbor?" Jesus told this story:

A man went down from Jerusalem to Jericho. He encountered thieves, who took off his clothes and beat him up, and left him near death.

Now it just so happened that a priest—a preacher—was also going down the same road. When he saw the injured man, he crossed over to the other side of the road and went on his way.

Likewise, a Levite—a teacher—came by that spot, saw the injured man, and crossed over to the other side of the road and went on his way.

A Samaritan who was on a journey came to where the man was. When he saw the man, he was moved to compassion.

The Samaritan went to the man and bandaged his wounds. Then he placed the man on his own donkey, took him to an inn, and took care of him.

The next day, the Samaritan took two full days' worth of wages and gave them to the innkeeper, saying, "Take care of him, and when I return, I will pay you back for any extra costs."

Jesus said, "What do you think? Which one of these three was a neighbor to the man who encountered thieves?"

Then the legal expert said, "The one who showed love and cared for him."

Jesus told him, "Go and do the same."

Role-Play Scenarios

Your older brother yells at you when you walk into his room without knocking. What do you do?

You are in line at school. The boy behind you starts calling another student bad names because she wears glasses. What do you do?

You and a friend are sitting together. Another classmate comes over and pinches your friend's arm. What do you do?

You are leaving gym class and notice a group of kids teasing and bullying a classmate. He is crying and asking for his gym bag back. What do you do?

You and your friend are playing ball. Another child comes over and takes your ball away. What do you do?

You see one of your friends point to a classmate and say, "She is ugly." What do you do?

You're walking down the hallway, and a teacher you don't like walks past you. The teacher accidently drops her books and papers all over the floor. What do you do?

You and some friends are playing soccer in the park. You notice that a child is on the sideline watching. What do you do?

Your mother has had a hard day at work and is tired. After dinner, you ask if she will play a game with you. She says that first she has to load the dishwasher, take out the trash, fold the clothes from the dryer, and make sure that your younger sister takes her bath. What do you do?

You are at a friend's house playing games on the computer. Your friend shows you a website that you know you are not allowed to use. What do you do?

3 God Is the Giver of Grace

Objectives

The children will:

- explore fears of failure or rejection.
- explore ways that God gave grace to Moses to stand up to Pharaoh.
- practice believing in themselves, as God believes in them.

Theme

We become unafraid when we receive God's gift of grace to forgive ourselves and to believe in ourselves.

Bible Verse

My grace is enough for you, because power is made perfect in weakness. (2 Corinthians 12:9)

Focus for the Teacher

Children have personal fears such as failing at school, disappointing their parents or teacher, or being rejected by others. These fears can be prevalent if children receive more criticism than positive affirmations. Children also need a chance to learn from their mistakes rather than being embarrassed or humiliated.

Moses had a holy encounter with God. He saw a burning bush that was not being consumed by the flames. He heard God's voice call his name. God said he had heard the cries of the Israelites and knew their pain. God was calling Moses to lead the Israelites out of Egypt. However, Moses replied that he had made mistakes in his life and wasn't important enough. He had a speech impediment, didn't know what to say, and was afraid no one would listen to him. Therefore he asked God to send someone else. In spite of Moses' fears, however, through God's grace Moses came to believe in himself and be unafraid. God gave Moses and his brother, Aaron, the courage to face Pharaoh and lead the Israelites out of Egypt. Moses let go of his fears and trusted the promise that God's grace and power would be with him.

Believe in ourselves and be unafraid.

The learning activities in this session will provide opportunities for the children to experience God's gift of grace. The children will practice taking a risk. They will explore how to forgive themselves and learn from their mistakes. They will explore ways to work together to accomplish a task.

Prayerfully consider what personal fears the children in your group might be experiencing. As a teacher, how can you affirm and applaud the children in your group? What are some ways you can help the children in your group believe in themselves and become unafraid? If there is a particularly difficult or troubled child in your group, how might you pray and shift your attitude about that child?

Explore Interest Groups

Be sure that adult leaders are waiting when the first child arrives. Greet and welcome the children. Get the children involved in an activity that interests them and introduces the theme for the day's activities.

Hit or Miss

- **Ask:** Who wins a basketball game?
- **Say:** The winner is the team with the highest score. The team who shoots the most balls into the basket.
- **Ask:** How many times do you think a player misses a shot before actually putting the ball into the basket?
- Encourage the children's answers.
- **Say:** We are going to play a game but with a twist.
- Divide the children into two teams.
- Have each team line up behind one of the taped lines.
- Give each team a beanbag.
- **Say:** Each team member takes a turn throwing the beanbag into the trash can. The team's score will be the number of times the team members miss the trash can. Whichever team has the fewest misses wins the game.
- Have the children play the game.
- **Say:** Now play again, but this time the team's score will be the number of times the team members get the beanbag into the trash can successfully. Whichever team gets the beanbag into the trash can the most times wins the game.
- Have the children play the game.
- **Ask:** How many missed the trash can? How many got the beanbag into the trash can?
- **Say:** Even the best basketball players miss more shots than they score. Sometimes we are so afraid of failing that we don't even try. Today, we are going to hear how Moses was afraid to lead the Israelites.

Prepare

✓ Provide two small trash cans, two beanbags, masking tape.

✓ Before class, create two "playing fields" using masking tape: tape two pieces of masking tape on the floor. Place a trash can 3′–4′ away from each masking tape line.

Prepare

✓ Using posterboard, cut out a large conversation bubble. In the center write, "If I couldn't fail..."

✓ Provide colored pencils and crayons.

If I Didn't Fail...

- **Say:** Sometimes we are afraid we will make a mistake or we will fail. I wonder what you would do if you knew that you would not fail. On the poster, write or draw your ideas.
- Encourage the children as they work together.
- **Say:** Sometimes we are afraid that we will be a failure. Today, we are going to learn about God's gift of grace. Through God's grace we can overcome our fear of being a failure.

Prepare

✓ Before class, create a simple obstacle course. Some ideas for activities: crawl under a table, bounce from one pillow to another, balance one foot on a stool, climb into a riding toy and go around a chair, walk a taped line on the floor, go down a slide, and so forth.

✓ Provide blindfolds.

Cooperative Obstacle Course

- **Ask:** What fears might keep you from completing a task?
- Encourage the children's answers.
- Have a volunteer walk alone through the obstacle course and practice the different tasks.
- **Ask:** What would happen if you had to do the obstacle course by yourself, but blindfolded?
- **Say:** Can anyone think of a way you could do the course blindfolded?
- Someone may come up with the idea of a helper who isn't blindfolded. If no one thinks of it, give the idea yourself.
- **Say:** Often it is hard to do a task by yourself. We can be successful, if we work together. Also, if we are afraid to do it by ourselves, a partner can help us. We are going to work with a partner to complete the course blindfolded.
- Divide children into teams of two.
- Blindfold one child in each team.
- Encourage the child who is not blindfolded to help the other child through the course.
- At the end of the course, have the blindfolded children give the blindfold to their partners and repeat the game, until everyone has had a chance to try both roles.
- **Ask:** When you were blindfolded, what tasks were easy? What was hard? How was your partner helpful?
- **Say:** We all have different strengths and abilities. When we work together it makes the task easier. Today, we are going to hear how Moses was afraid to lead the Israelites, but God sent Moses a partner to help him.

Grace Is . . .

- **Say:** Today, we will learn about God's gift of grace by doing a crossword puzzle.
- Give each child and copy of **Reproducible 3a: Grace Is...**
- **Say:** Read the definitions, then look for the Bible verse and fill in the blank. You may work together if you need help.
- Assist the children as needed.
- **Ask:** How do these words help us understand God's grace?
- Encourage the children's answers.

✓ Provide copies of **Reproducible 3a: Grace Is...,** found at the end of the lesson.

✓ Provide Bibles and pencils.

Answer Key:

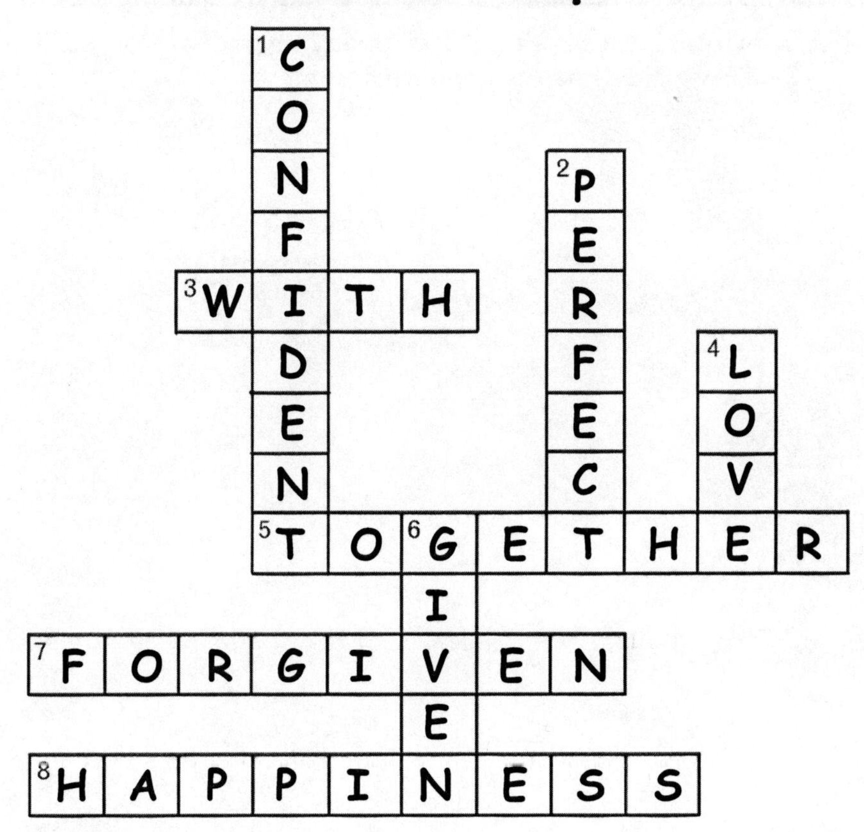

Large Group

Bring all the children together to experience the Bible story. Use a bell to alert the children to the large group time.

Prepare

✓ Make two copies of **Reproducible 3b: No, Not Me!** found at the end of the lesson.

✓ Before class, invite two strong readers in your class—one playing Moses and one playing God—to read the story of Moses and the burning bush from the reproducible.

✓ You might want to bring some simple costumes or props for the readers to use.

No, Not Me!

- **Say:** Today we are going to hear a story about Moses.
- **Ask:** What do you remember about Moses?
- Encourage the children's answers.
- **Say:** There was one time when Moses was afraid. He was afraid that he could not lead the Israelites. Listen to Moses' conversation with God. Listen for all the ways Moses was afraid. Count how many times Moses told God, "No."
- Have the readers tell the story of Moses and the burning bush.
- **Ask:** Why was Moses afraid? How many times did Moses tell God, "No"? How did Moses overcome his fears?

God's Gift of Grace

- **Ask:** From our last two weeks, what two gifts from God help us be unafraid? (Courage and love) When has God given you courage this week? When have you loved someone this week? Who remembers our two memory verses?
- **Say:** Today we learn about a third gift from God: the gift of grace. God sent us the gift of grace through Jesus Christ, who gave his life for us.
- Show the markerboard and read this week's Bible verse together: "My grace is enough for you, because power is made perfect in weakness." (2 Corinthians 12:9)
- Say: God takes our fears and weakness and helps us overcome them. We call this grace. Through grace, God used Moses' fears and weakness to be a perfect leader for the Israelites.
- **Ask:** What can happen when we receive God's gift of grace?
- **Say:** We don't have to be afraid. God is always with us. God always loves us. God forgives us when we make a mistake. God gives us courage and confidence. God believes in us and gives us the power to believe in ourselves even when we are afraid.
- Write the letters G-R-A-C-E vertically on the markerboard.
- **Say:** Let's see if we can work together to come up with a word or phrase for each letter that describes how we can be unafraid through God's gift of grace.
- Encourage the children to name words. Some examples: **G**od loves us; **R**isk-taker; **A**ccepts us; **C**ourageous; **E**xcited to try new tasks.
- Read the Bible verse together one more time: "My grace is enough for you, because power is made perfect in weakness." (2 Corinthians 12:9)

Prepare

✓ Provide a markerboard and markers.

✓ Write on the markerboard this week's Bible verse: "My grace is enough for you, because power is made perfect in weakness." (2 Corinthians 12:9)

Small Groups

Divide the children into small groups. You may organize the groups around age levels or around readers and nonreaders. Keep the groups small, with a maximum of ten children in each group. You may need to have more than one group at each age level.

Prepare

✓ Provide posterboard for each child, along with magazines, scissors, glue, crayons, and markers.

✓ Bring a hand mirror for yourself.

Young Children

- **Ask:** What have you learned today about God's gift of grace?
- Encourage children to share their answers.
- **Say:** This week's memory verse is long. Let's see if we can memorize just part of it: "made perfect in weakness."
- Have the children repeat the words and practice them until they are memorized.
- **Ask:** What do you think these words mean?
- **Say:** Even though Moses was afraid, God believed in him. God takes all your weakness, mistakes, doubts about yourself, and fears and makes you perfect. God believes in you. In fact, God thinks all of you are awesome!
- Give each child a posterboard.
- **Say:** Use the magazines to cut out pictures and words that show how awesome you are! You can also use the crayons and markers to write words or draw pictures.
- Have the children create their "I Am Awesome!" posters.
- Affirm and applaud the different ways the children are awesome.
- **Say:** Take your poster home and hang in your bedroom. Anytime you make a mistake or feel you can't do something, look at your poster. Remember that God believes in you. Remember that God thinks you are awesome! Remember that through God's gift of grace you are made perfect in weakness.
- Invite the children to sit in a circle.
- **Say:** I am going to hold this hand mirror in front of my face and look at myself. Then I will name one way that I can be perfect in weakness, with God's help.
- Share one way that you can be perfect in weakness. (Work with others, be confident, forgive my friend, try something new, learn from my mistakes, and so forth.)
- **Say:** I am going to pass the mirror around the circle. As you look at yourself, share one way God can make you perfect in weakness.
- Pass the mirror around the circle.
- Encourage and prompt the children.
- **Pray:**

  Thank you, God, for believing in us. Thank you for making us perfect in our weakness.
- **Say:** All God's children said, "Amen."

Older Children

- **Ask:** What have you learned today about God's gift of grace?
- Encourage children to share their answers.
- **Ask:** Who remembers today's Bible memory verse? It's a hard one.
- Applaud the child or children who remember.
- Give each child a piece of paper with one word of the verse written on it. If there are too few or too many children to give each child one word, have them work together.
- Have the children work to put the Bible verse in order.
- When the Bible verse is completed, have the children read it together: "My grace is enough for you, because power is made perfect in weakness." (2 Corinthians 12:9)
- **Say:** Even though Moses was afraid, God believed in him. God believes in you.
- Pair the children. Ask each pair to choose an "I Can!" slogan from the basket.
- **Say:** God believes in each of us, so we can believe in ourselves. Through God's gift of grace, we have the power to turn our fears and negative thoughts into positive thoughts. Instead of saying "I can't," we can say "I can!"
- Invite each pair to read the "I Can!" slogan they chose from the basket, pausing to discuss what each slogan means. Encourage the class to think of examples from their own lives.
- **Say:** Today we're going to pray a different kind of prayer. We can pray it with our bodies. When I pray a sentence, copy my action. Let us pray:

  Thank you, God for your gift of grace.

  (Raise arms above shoulders)

  You believe in me, so I can believe in myself.

  (Place hands on your chest)

  Even when I am afraid, you are with me.

  (Outstretch arms, palms facing up)

  Give me your power, to be made perfect in you.

  (Clinch fists in a power stance)

  Amen.

Prepare

✓ Write each word of this week's Bible verse on an 8½x11 sheet of paper: "My grace is enough for you, because power is made perfect in weakness."

✓ Copy **Reproducible 3c: I Can!** found at the end of the lesson. Cut out each "I Can!" slogan, fold, and place in a basket.

Reproducible 3a

Grace Is...

Look up each Bible verse in the definitions below and fill in the blank. Then write your answer in the correct box on the puzzle.
(Note: These verses are from the Common English Bible. If you don't have a copy, you can find the Bible online.)

Across

3. God said, I'll be _____ you. (Exodus 3:12)
5. We work _____ with him. (2 Corinthians 6:1)
7. I assure you that human beings will be _____ for everything. (Mark 3:28)
8. I find _____ in him. (Matthew 3:17)

Down

1. This is why we are _____. (2 Corinthians 1:12)
2. My grace is enough for you because…made _____ in weakness. (2 Corinthians 12:9)
4. He did this because of the great _____ that he has for us. (Ephesians 2:5)
6. God's grace that was _____ to you in Christ Jesus. (1 Corinthians 1:4)

No, Not Me!
(Based on Exodus 3:1-12)

Moses: (Astonished) What is that? A bush is on fire but isn't burning up!

God: Moses! Moses!

Moses: No, not me! God, why are you calling me?

God: Moses! Moses! Don't come any closer. Take off your sandals. You are standing on holy ground. Remember I am the God of Abraham, of Isaac, and of Jacob.

Moses: No, not me! God, I'm afraid.

God: I have seen how hard the slave masters work the Israelites. You will go back to Egypt and be their leader! You will lead them out of Egypt to Canaan.

Moses: No, not me! God, I don't want to go.

God: I will be with you.

Moses: No, not me! God, what will I say to them? They won't listen to me.

God: I will tell you what to say.

Moses: No, not me! God, I don't speak very well.

God: I will send your brother, Aaron, to go with you.

Moses: No, not me! God, choose another leader. He will be better than me!

God: I believe in you. My grace is enough for you. I will give you courage.

Moses: God, if you trust me and promise to be with me, I will go and lead the Israelites out of Egypt.

Reproducible 3c

I Can!

Learn from my mistakes

Welcome challenges

Work to improve

Not blame others

Not be afraid to fail

Use different ideas

Forgive myself

Be inspired by others' success

Overcome obstacles

Learn new things

4 God Is the Giver of Hope

Objectives

The children will:

- explore their fears of being home alone, of moving, or of seeing tragic news on television or the Internet.
- see themselves as part of God's dream of a new heaven and a new earth.
- practice giving their fears to God by serving others.

Theme

We become unafraid when we receive God's gift of hope to be part of a new heaven and a new earth.

Bible Verse

Look! I'm creating a new heaven and a new earth. (Isaiah 65:17)

Focus for the Teacher

Children are sometimes afraid of being home alone. If children move to a new home, they may be anxious about making new friends or getting used to a new school, neighborhood, or church. If there has been tragic news in your community, children may be frightened about how it will affect them.

Children, like all of us, experience fear. One way to be unafraid is to give those fears to God. When we use our imagination, we release our fears by joining with God to envision a new way of seeing our circumstances. For example, instead of being frightened about going to a new church, we can imagine meeting new friends there. In imagining positive outcomes, we become part of God's dream of a new heaven and a new earth.

Another way to release our fears to God is by turning our attention to serving others. When we switch our attention to someone else, we no longer have time to think about our own fears. At the end of the session, we will be doing a low-cost service project. Through our service with others, we become part of God's dream of a new heaven and a new earth.

Give our fears to God.

Whenever we seek to be part of God's dream, we are living with hope. Even when something terrible happens, God is with us. Working together, we can bring hope for a new heaven and a new earth.

Think about the children in your group. Have any of them experienced the fear of being home alone, of moving, or of traumatic news in the community? How have you and the children used your imaginations to envision a new set of circumstances? How have you and your church responded to people when they are in frightening situations? What are some concrete ways in which children might serve others at church? at school? in the neighborhood?

Explore Interest Groups

Be sure that adult leaders are waiting when the first child arrives. Greet and welcome the children. Get the children involved in an activity that interests them and introduces the theme for the day's activities.

Capture Your Fears

- **Say:** Today we're going to be talking about our fears and how we can tame them. Let's start by each thinking of something we're afraid of. Don't speak it; just think it.
- **Say:** Now we're going to use any of these craft supplies on the table to draw or build an imaginary character or machine to tame our fears.
- Give time for the children to work on their creations.
- If they wish, the children can name their creations.
- When the children finish, let them share their creations with the group if they are willing.
- **Say:** Take your creation home. Anytime you're afraid, write your fear and give it to your creation so the creation will tame it.

Prepare

✓ Provide a variety of art materials on the table. Items might includeboxes of different sizes, cans, yarn, buttons, ribbon, sequins, chenille stems, construction paper, crayons, markers, scissors, and glue.

Praying with Color

- Give each child a copy of **Reproducible 4a: Praying with Color**.
- **Say:** You've experienced different feelings and fears in your lifetime. Look at the color key. Each color represents a different feeling or fear.
- Read through the color key with the group.
- **Say:** Whenever we are afraid, we can give our fears to God by praying. One way to pray is to color. Fill up the body with colors that represent your feelings and fears.
- As the children pray and color, play soft, meditative music.
- Invite the children to share their pictures. Engage the children in conversation about how the colors show their feelings and fears.
- **Say:** Prayer is one way to give our fears to God.

Prepare

✓ Provide copies of **Reproducible 4a: Praying with Color,** found at the end of this lesson.

✓ Provide crayons or colored pencils, meditative music, and a device to play the music.

Prepare

✓ Provide a variety of items useful in serving others, such as a soup pot, cell phone, shovel, coat, musical instrument, football, adhesive bandage, coffee cup, bread, envelope, and so forth.

✓ Provide a sheet of paper and pencils or pens.

Useful to Serve Others

- Show the children all the items you have gathered.
- **Say:** All these items have something in common. Everything here can be used to serve others.
- Pick up two or three items and have the children brainstorm all the ways each object can be used to serve others.
- Divide the children into groups of three or four.
- Assign one person in each group to record the group's thoughts.
- Create a story about someone who is afraid. One idea: "I have new neighbors. They just moved into the house down the street. They don't know anyone that lives here. They are afraid about making new friends. Their children are afraid to start a new school."
- **Say:** Your group has two minutes to come up with ways you can use these objects to serve this family and help them be unafraid.
- After two minutes, invite the groups to share their best two ideas.
- **Say:** As you can see, there are many ways to serve others. Whenever we focus on serving others, we don't have time to think about our own fears.

Large Group

Bring all the children together to experience the Bible story. Use a bell to alert the children to the large group time.

Would You Rather

- **Say:** I am going to read a question. You have to decide what you would rather do. If you would rather do the first choice, stand near sign #1. If you would rather do the second choice, stand near sign #2. You have to make a choice even if you don't like either choice.
- Read the first question. ("Would you rather eat grapes or apples?")
- **Say:** If you would rather eat grapes—the first choice—go stand near sign #1. If you would rather eat apples—the second choice—go stand near sign #2.
- Continue reading each question and have all the children make a choice.
- Periodically, invite the children to share why they made a particular choice.
- **Say:** I wonder what kind of world God would rather we live in.

Prepare

✓ The leader will need a copy of **Reproducible 4b: Would You Rather**, found at the end of the lesson.

✓ On one piece of newsprint or large sheet of paper write a large #1, and on another piece of newsprint or paper write a large #2. Tape the papers on opposite walls.

Prayer of Hope

- **Say:** When we pray, we can give our fears to God. We can ask God to help us use our imaginations to come up with ideas, so we will be unafraid. God can also show us how to serve others and give hope to others.
- Show children the lyrics to *"Canto de Espranza"* ("Song of Hope") on the markerboard.
- Teach the hymn, in English, in Spanish, or in both.
- Invite the children to sing the hymn as a prayer.
- Dismiss children to their small groups.

Prepare

✓ Use the Internet to locate the lyrics to *"Canto de Esperanza"* ("Song of Hope"), and write them on a markerboard, in English, in Spanish, or in both.

✓ *Hint*: If this hymn is not familiar, invite a musician to teach the song to the class.

Prepare

✓ Write this week's Bible verse on a markerboard: "Look! I'm creating a new heaven and a new earth" (Isaiah 65:17).

Gift of Hope

- **Ask:** Who remembers the Bible verse we learned about God's gift of courage? God's gift of love? God's gift of grace?
- Prompt children as they remember.
- **Ask:** How has God been with you this week? How have you had courage? love? grace?
- **Say:** Today's gift is hope.
- **Ask:** What do you think hope means?
- **Say:** Another way of saying it is that hope means to expect that God's dream for a new heaven and a new earth is possible.
- Read today's Bible verse together from the markerboard: "Look! I'm creating a new heaven and a new earth."
- **Say:** Whenever we are afraid, we can do two things to help create a new heaven and a new earth. First, we can use our imaginations and come up with ways not to be afraid.
- **Ask:** If you are afraid of moving, how can you imagine being unafraid? If you are afraid of being home alone, how can you imagine being unafraid?
- Continue to name things the children are afraid of and ask them to imagine how they can be unafraid.
- **Say:** A second thing we can do instead of thinking about our fears is to work with God to serve others and be part of God's dream for a new heaven and a new earth. We can give hope to others.
- **Ask:** How does serving others create a new heaven and a new earth?
- Encourage the children to come up with ideas.
- **Say:** Whenever we are serving others, we don't have time to think about our fears. Let's read our Bible verse together three more times, but let's imagine that I am a volume control slider. When I am standing over here (move all the way to your right side) the volume needs to be very soft. As I walk across the room, the volume increases, and when I am standing over here (move all the way to your left side) the volume is very loud.
- Say the verse three more times as you control the volume with your position.

Small Groups

Divide the children into small groups. You may organize the groups around age levels or around readers and nonreaders. Keep the groups small, with a maximum of ten children in each group. You may need to have more than one group at each age level.

Young Children

- **Ask:** Who remembers our memory verse today?
- Prompt the children, as needed, to remember "Look! I'm creating a new heaven and a new earth."
- **Say:** Whenever we serve others, we are working with God to create a new heaven and new earth. We also show others God's gift of hope.
- **Ask:** If your grandparents are around and you see them, what do you talk about with them? What words or pictures might bring a smile to your grandparents?
- **Say:** Sometimes older adults can be lonely, especially if it's too difficult to get out and see friends or family. We are going to provide hope to some older persons in our community who are not able to come to church and who might be lonely. We are going to create cards that say, "Thinking of you."
- Give each child a sheet of card stock.
- Tell the children to fold their paper in half.
- Fold the paper in half again to create a card.
- Encourage the children to write the words "Thinking of you" on the front of the card and decorate the card using the colored pencils or crayons.
- Help the children write a message on the inside of their card and sign their name.
- **Say:** We will deliver these cards to older adults in our community. These cards will bring a smile to the adults who receive them and will remind them that we care about them.
- **Pray:**

  Jesus, thank you for showing us how to be unafraid by serving others. Be with those who will receive our cards. May it remind them that we are thinking of them and that we care. Amen.

Prepare

✓ Provide white card stock, colored pencils, and crayons.

✓ *Optional*: Also provide stickers and templates of different shapes.

✓ *Tip*: Determine how to deliver cards to members of your congregation who are homebound or to a retirement center in your community.

Prepare

- ✓ Arrange in advance to provide items to a local community shelter for the homeless.
- ✓ Provide a variety of items that would be helpful to people experiencing homelessness: socks, lip balm, deodorant, toothbrushes, toothpaste, wet wipes, adhesive bandages, beef jerky, and so forth.
- ✓ *Tip*: The children will be using these to each fill a "blessing sock" during the activity, so make sure you bring enough items to fill everyone's sock.
- ✓ If you choose not to purchase the items yourself, divide the list among the children. Send an e-mail to the parents telling them that their children will be making blessing socks for the homeless. Ask them to provide a specific item and indicate the specific number needed. You might also partner with an adult class to donate the items for the children to assemble.
- ✓ Once you've gathered the items, spread them out on a table, assembly-line fashion, before class starts.

Older Children

- **Ask:** Who remembers our memory verse today?
- Prompt the children, as needed, to remember: "Look! I'm creating a new heaven and a new earth."
- **Say:** One of God's dreams is that everyone will have a place to live and food to eat. We can be co-creators with God to create a new heaven and a new earth as we serve and offer hope to those who don't have homes.
- **Say:** Today we're going to offer hope by making blessing socks. These are socks that will bless the people who receive them.
- Give each child a pair of socks.
- Have the children roll up one sock and put it in the other sock.
- Have the children walk down the assembly line, filling their sock with one each of the items.
- Repeat until all the socks are filled.
- Follow through with your arrangements to deliver the blessing socks to a community shelter for the homeless. If possible, ask a person who is homeless or someone who works with the homeless to share with the children what it is like to be homeless.
- Have the children form a circle.
- **Ask:** In addition to blessing socks, what are some ways that you can serve other people this week?
- Encourage children to share their ideas.
- **Say:** When we are serving others, we can forget our own fears and become unafraid. We are partners with God to create a new heaven and a new earth.
- Invite a child to offer a closing prayer.

Praying with Color

Color Key:

Red	=	Angry
Orange	=	Excited
Yellow	=	Scared
Green	=	Happy
Blue	=	Sad
Purple	=	Thoughtful

Would You Rather

1. Would you rather eat grapes or apples?

2. Would you rather live in a hut or an igloo?

3. Would you rather play ball or dance?

4. Would you rather eat pizza at home or go to a movie?

5. Would you rather be sick or be afraid?

6. Would you rather play by yourself or with the new kid in your neighborhood?

7. Would you rather touch a lion or a snake?

8. Would you rather live a long life feeling miserable or a shorter life feeling happy?

9. Would you rather overcome your biggest fear or accomplish your biggest dream?

10. Would you rather call God on the phone or write a letter to God?

5 God Is the Giver of Peace

Objectives

The children will:

- explore their fears of storms and natural disasters.
- experience the story of Jesus calming the storm.
- practice trusting God through prayer.

Theme

We become unafraid when we trust God and receive God's gift of peace.

Bible Verse

I will trust and won't be afraid. (Isaiah 12:2)

Focus for the Teacher

Children can be afraid of storms, particularly if your community has experienced a recent thunderstorm or natural disaster. They can become anxious listening to news about a natural disaster.

While Jesus and his friends traveled across the sea, Jesus was asleep in the back of the boat. A storm came up, creating monstrous waves sloshing over the boat. The disciples became afraid they would drown. They awoke Jesus, begging him to rescue them. Jesus asked his friends why they were afraid. Jesus then got up and ordered the winds and waves to be calm. God gives us a sense of peace even when storms threaten us.

Trust God and be unafraid.

In this session, the children will experience trusting God to be with us. We will affirm that God is awesome even when we see lightning or when we see first responders helping others. We will affirm that we can trust that God is always with us.

The children will learn that prayer is a conversation with God. Whenever we pray, we can express our gratitude that God is always with us. We can express our fears. We can listen for the positive thoughts that bubble up in our hearts. Throughout the session, children will have opportunities to practice different ways of praying.

Who taught you how to pray? How is prayer important in your life? Think of recent experiences in your own life, in the lives of the children, and in your community that show that God will always be with us.

Explore Interest Groups

Be sure that adult leaders are waiting when the first child arrives. Greet and welcome the children. Get the children involved in an activity that interests them and introduces the theme for the day's activities.

Glitter Bottle

- **Ask:** What have you been afraid of this week?
- Encourage the children's stories.
- **Say:** Today we are going to make a "glitter bottle" that you can use when you are afraid.
- Give each child an empty water bottle and cap.
- Help them fill the bottle halfway with warm water. Make sure the water is warm, so the glitter (see below) does not clump.
- Add glitter.
- Add 1-2 tablespoons of the hair gel mix you made before class, to make the water dense.
- If needed, add more warm water to fill the bottle, then screw on the cap.
- **Say:** Shake your bottle. Create a storm of glitter swirling.
- Have the children shake their bottles and watch the glitter swirl.
- **Say:** Put your bottle down. Take some deep breaths, and watch what happens to the swirling glitter.
- **Ask:** What happened to the glitter?
- **Say**: Today in our large group time, we will hear a story of how Jesus calmed the fearful disciples. You can be calm, too. Take the filled bottle home with you. Whenever you are afraid, shake your bottle. As you watch the glitter settle, you can take several deep breaths. This will help you be calm and unafraid.

Prepare

✓ Provide a half-pint water bottle and cap for each child, warm water, multicolored glitter, hair gel, and a hot glue gun.

✓ Before class, mix 1½ cups warm water with ¾ cup hair gel for every 12 students.

Hidden Peace

- **Say:** Today we are going to learn about God's gift of peace.
- **Ask:** What does peace mean?
- Encourage the children's answers.
- Give each child a copy of **Reproducible 5a: Hidden Peace**.
- Read the words at the bottom of the puzzle.
- Discuss ways these words describe peace.
- **Say:** These words help us describe peace. See if you can find the words hidden in the puzzle. Some words will be horizontal, vertical, or backward.
- Have the children complete their puzzle.

Prepare

✓ Provide copies of **Reproducible 5a: Hidden Peace,** found at the end of the lesson.

✓ *Tip*: An answer key for this activity can be found on page 63.

✓ Provide pencils.

Prepare

✓ Provide colored index cards, markers, crayons, and stickers.

Prayer Cards

- **Ask:** When are you afraid?
- Encourage the children to talk about their fears.
- **Say:** When we pray, God can help us be unafraid.
- Give each child several index cards.
- Have each child write the word "PRAY" in large letters on each card.
- Encourage the children to decorate their cards.
- **Say**: When you take these cards home, put them around your house in places where you will see them frequently. When you see a card, take a moment and say a prayer. The prayer doesn't need to be long or complicated. It can be as simple as, "God, thank you for this day," or "Help me be unafraid." We can pray about anything.

Prepare

✓ Designate a safe, soft area to play.

Learning to Trust

- Have the children stand in a circle.
- **Say:** We are going to work together as a team to trust one another. The person in the center of the circle will stand and fall backward, trusting everyone else in the circle to catch him or her.
- Choose a volunteer to stand in the center of the circle.
- Tell the child in the center to stand straight, arms by her or his side, and be stiff and rigid.
- Once everyone is ready, tell the child in the center to count to three.
- On the count of three the child in the center will fall backward.
- The children in the circle will catch the child and keep the child from falling.
- The circle of children will gently pass the child in the middle around the circle.
- Once the child has been passed around the circle, gently guide the child back to the center and help him or her stand upright again.
- Repeat, allowing all the children to have a turn in the center.
- **Say:** We had to trust our friends in the circle to not let us fall. We are going to hear today how the disciples learned to trust Jesus, even when they were afraid.

Large Group

Bring all the children together to experience the Bible story. Use a bell to alert the children to the large group time.

Rainbow Tambourine

- **Ask:** When can we see a rainbow? How do you feel when you see a rainbow?
- Give each child a paper plate.
- Color the paper plate. Start with red around the outside rim of the paper plate. Then add, in order, a circle of orange, yellow, green, blue, and a small inner circle of purple.
- Fold the paper plate in half with the colored side showing.
- Pair an older child with a younger child so that they can work together.
- With a pencil, mark along the outer arc about an inch apart.
- Punch a hole at the markings. Make sure that both sides of the plate are punched through.
- Tie one end of the ribbon through the first hole in the plate. Thread on a bell. Thread the ribbon through the next hole in the plate. Thread on a bell. Repeat until you reach the last hole, and tie the ribbon to the plate. *Tip*: The bells need to be loose to jingle.
- **Say:** No matter how scary a storm can be, when we see a rainbow we remember that God is with us. We will use the tambourines during our story time.

Prepare

✓ Provide paper plates, markers or crayons, pencils, hole punch, small jingle bells, and red ribbon cut into strips.

Calming the Storm

- Invite the children to sit in a circle.
- **Ask:** When have you been afraid this week? When have you been afraid of storms?
- Encourage the children to share their stories.
- **Say:** Jesus and his disciples were caught in a storm, and the disciples were afraid. I need your help to tell a story. It's called "Calming the Storm."
- Before reading the story, help the children practice the motions listed with each line.
- **Say:** As I read the story, follow my motions.
- Read the story on **Reproducible 5b: Calming the Storm**, and encourage the children to make the motion that goes with each line.

Prepare

✓ The leader will need a copy of **Reproducible 5b: Calming the Storm**, found at the end of the lesson.

✓ Provide the tambourines created earlier.

- **Ask:** How do you think the disciples felt when they were so scared and Jesus was asleep?
- How do you think Jesus' voice sounded when he told the wind and waves to be still? Do you think it was loud and forceful, or gentle like he was calming a baby?
- Try saying, "Peace, be still!" in different ways.
- **Ask:** What can be scary in a storm? How can we be thankful for a storm?
- Help the children realize that watching lightning from a safe place can be awesome, and afterward storms can create beautiful rainbows. Remind the children that we can be unafraid because God is always with us, even in storms.

Prepare

✓ Write this week's Bible verse on a markerboard: "I will trust and won't be afraid." (Isaiah 12:2)

Gift of Peace

- **Ask:** What gifts from God help us be unafraid? This past week, how have you had courage? love? grace? hope?
- Encourage the children to share their stories.
- **Say:** Today's gift is peace.
- **Ask:** What do you think *peace* means?
- Use words from the word search to describe peace.
- **Say:** There was peace when Jesus stopped the wind and waves. There is peace when we trust God is with us. When we are at peace, we can be unafraid.
- Read the Bible verse together: "I will trust and won't be afraid" (Isaiah 12:2).
- **Say:** Being afraid of storms is a natural way to feel. Storms are powerful. Storms are scary. But we can hug ourselves (*Hug yourself!*) and imagine that God is with us, holding us safe until the storm passes. Parents will also hug us! We can pray and tell God our fears. We can feel peace, trusting that God is with us.
- Read the Bible verse together, "I will trust and won't be afraid" (Isaiah 12:2).

Trust God

- **Say:** Prayer is a conversation with God. When we pray, we can talk to God but we can also listen to God.
- **Ask:** When do you pray? What do you usually pray about?
- **Say:** When we pray, we can be thankful that God is always with us. We can tell God that we are afraid. We can feel God's peace.
- Have the children stand in a circle.
- **Say:** We often think of folding our hands and bowing our heads when we pray. That's fine, but there are many other prayer positions. In fact, there is no wrong way to pray! Right now, we are going to pray several different ways. I will begin by giving a prayer position. Once everyone is in that position, I will say a short prayer. We will repeat the process several times.
- Lead the children in prayer, giving the following prayer positions and the corresponding prayers:

(Head bowed and hands folded)
God, we thank you that we can pray to you about anything.

(Hands raised high in the air)
God, we thank you that we can pray when we are joyful and excited.

(Shoulders slumped, sad face)
God, we thank you that you hear our prayers when we are sad or afraid.

(Kneeling)
God, help us remember to talk with you often.

(Sports huddle)
God, we thank you that we can pray to you wherever we are.

(Standing, hands spread out to the side)
God, we thank you that we can pray to you about anything!

(Sitting)
God, we thank you for hearing our prayers. Amen.

Small Groups

Divide the children into small groups. You may organize the groups around age levels or around readers and nonreaders. Keep the groups small, with a maximum of ten children in each group. You may need to have more than one group at each age level.

Prepare

✓ Provide a ball.

Young Children

- **Say:** This is our last week. We have been learning how to be unafraid.
- **Ask:** Who remembers God's five gifts that help us be unafraid?
- Prompt the children to remember courage, love, grace, hope, and peace.
- Have the children stand in a circle.
- **Say:** I am going to share one way that God's gift of courage helps me be unafraid. Then I will pass this ball to another person who will share one way that helps them. We will continue to pass the ball around the circle until everyone has had a chance to share.
- Encourage and prompt the children as needed.
- Continue to play until the group has shared ideas for each of God's gifts: courage, love, grace, hope, and peace.
- **Say:** We are going to stand in a circle and pray together. We can pray with our eyes open. We are first going to tell God about the things that make us want to say, "Thanks."
- Have children share their prayers of thanks.
- **Say:** Next, we are going to pray for those things that make us want to say, "Help."
- Have the children share their prayers of help.
- **Say:** And all God's people said: Amen.

Older Children

- **Say:** This is our last week. We have been learning how to be unafraid.
- **Ask:** Who remembers God's five gifts that help us be unafraid?
- Prompt the children to remember courage, love, grace, hope, and peace.
- **Ask:** How is courage helpful when you are afraid? love? grace? hope? peace?
- Encourage the children as they share their ideas for each gift.
- When we are afraid, remembering God's gifts and our memory Bible verses will help us be unafraid. We can remember that God is with us and gives us ways to be unafraid.
- Give each child a copy of **Reproducible 5c: Unafraid**, which shows five cards—one each for the five gifts. (Don't cut the cards out yet. Give each child a copy of the sheet that shows all five cards.)
- Take turns reading the words on each of the cards.
- Have the children decorate their cards with words or pictures that will help them remember the Bible verse.
- Have the children cut out the cards.
- Help the children stack their five cards together and hole punch each card in the upper left corner.
- Hand out the rings, and have the children bind their five cards together using a ring.
- **Say:** You can take your cards home, and whenever you are afraid, you can remember what we have learned so that you will be unafraid.
- Have the children stand in a circle.
- **Say:** We've worked hard to remember our memory verses. Let's see how many we can remember.
- **Ask:** Which verse reminds us of God's gift of courage?
- As a group say together the Bible verse, "Don't fear, because I am with you."
- Continue to ask and say the Bible verse for each of God's gifts.
- **Say:** Think back on the past five weeks. Decide on one thing you want to tell God about these sessions in a prayer.
- Pause and give time for the children to think.
- **Say:** We can pray with our eyes open. We will go around the circle and give everyone a chance to pray. If you choose, you can pass by squeezing the person's hand next to you.
- Pray, giving every child a chance to participate.
- **Say:** And all God's people said: Amen.

Prepare

✓ Make copies on a variety of colored card stock of **Reproducible 5c: Unafraid**, found at the end of the lesson.

✓ Provide colored pencils, fine-tip markers, scissors, hole punch, and a ring for each child like those used in a ring binder.

Reproducible 5a

Hidden Peace

Find the words hidden in the puzzle.
The words may be horizontal, vertical, or backward.

L	V	G	I	U	C	O	M	K	D	B	V
Z	A	Q	A	N	Y	C	J	V	D	V	F
I	F	A	O	D	S	E	E	M	S	Q	T
W	F	C	W	E	Y	A	C	N	S	E	N
U	Z	G	S	R	C	S	N	F	E	J	E
E	W	J	T	S	M	E	E	O	N	L	M
H	S	T	I	T	T	F	L	Y	E	J	E
A	I	R	L	A	F	I	I	T	V	E	E
R	M	U	L	N	T	R	S	I	I	M	R
M	L	S	N	D	A	E	I	N	G	L	G
O	M	T	E	I	E	F	E	E	R	A	A
N	F	Z	S	N	R	F	L	R	O	C	E
Y	E	A	S	G	U	A	L	E	F	L	A
G	O	O	D	W	I	L	L	S	S	P	K
U	C	O	M	P	R	O	M	I	S	E	E

AGREEMENT
CALM
CEASEFIRE
COMPROMISE
FORGIVENESS
GOODWILL
HARMONY
SERENITY
SILENCE
STILLNESS
TRUST
UNDERSTANDING

Calming the Storm
(Based on Matthew 8:23-27)

Jesus got into a boat with his disciples. He went to the back of the boat and fell asleep.

Then, all of a sudden, rain started to fall. It started as just a drizzle.

(Snap your fingers together to make a rain sound.)

Soon, it became a rhythmic patter of rain. The thunder clapped!

(Clap your hands.)

It kept raining and raining and raining! Lightning streaked across the sky. Thunder boomed!

(Alternate clapping your hands and periodically clapping your legs for thunder.)

The huge storm rose up! Waves sloshed into the boat!

(Shake tambourines.)

Jesus was asleep!

(Continue shaking tambourines.)

The disciples ran to Jesus and said, "Lord, rescue us! We're going to drown!" Jesus said to them, "Why are you afraid, you people of weak faith?"

(Continue shaking tambourines.)

Then Jesus got up and said to the winds and the lake, "Peace, be still!" And there was a great calm.

(Stop shaking tambourines. Be silent and still.)

The disciples weren't afraid anymore. They knew Jesus was with them.

Unafraid

COURAGE

Don't fear, because
I am with you.

(Isaiah 41:10)

LOVE

Love your neighbor
as yourself.

(Luke 10:27)

GRACE

My grace is enough for you,
because power is made
perfect in weakness.

(2 Corinthians 12:9)

HOPE

Look! I'm creating a
new heaven and a
new earth.

(Isaiah 65:17)

PEACE

I will trust and
won't be afraid

(Isaiah 12:2)

Answer Key for Reproducible 5a: Hidden Peace

L	V	G	I	U	C	O	M	K	D	B	V
Z	A	Q	A	N	Y	C	J	V	D	V	F
I	F	A	O	D	S	E	E	M	S	Q	T
W	F	C	W	E	Y	A	C	N	S	E	N
U	Z	G	S	R	C	S	N	F	E	J	E
E	W	J	T	S	M	E	E	O	N	L	M
H	S	T	I	T	T	F	L	Y	E	J	E
A	I	R	L	A	F	I	I	T	V	E	E
R	M	U	L	N	T	R	S	I	I	M	R
M	L	S	N	D	A	E	I	N	G	L	G
O	M	T	E	I	E	F	E	E	R	A	A
N	F	Z	S	N	R	F	L	R	O	C	E
Y	E	A	S	G	U	A	L	E	F	L	A
G	O	O	D	W	I	L	L	S	S	P	K
U	C	O	M	P	R	O	M	I	S	E	E

CPSIA information can be obtained
at www.ICGtesting.com
Printed in the USA
LVOW09s0542310118
564644LV00004B/25/P

9 781501 853845